# The Glory of God's Will

## Elisabeth Elliot

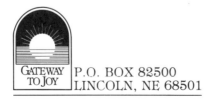

GATEWAY TO JOY   P.O. BOX 82500
LINCOLN, NE 68501

*The Glory of God's Will*

This material was given as a talk to
the Inter-Varsity Student Missionary Convention,
Urbana, Illinois, in December, 1976.

The Good News Broadcasting Association, Inc.
15,000 printed to date—1995
(1155-074—5M—65)
ISBN 0-8474-1195-8

Cover photo: H. Armstrong Roberts

Printed in the United States of America

# 1

## *The Master's Will*

High in the mountains of North Wales in a place called Llanymawddwy lives a shepherd named John Jones with his wife Mari and his black and white dog Mack. I stood one misty summer morning in the window of the farmhouse watching John on horseback herding the sheep with Mack. A few cows were quietly chewing their cud in a nearby corner while perhaps a hundred sheep moved across the dewy meadow toward the pens where they were to be dipped. Mack, a champion Scottish collie, was in his glory. He came from a long line of working dogs, and he had sheep in his blood. This was what he was made for, this was what he had been trained to do, and it was a marvelous thing to see him circling to the right, circling to the left, barking, crouching, racing along, herding a stray sheep here, nipping at a stubborn one there, his eyes always glued to the sheep, his ears listening for the tiny metal whistle from his master which I couldn't hear.

Mari took me to the pens to watch what John had to do there. When all the animals had been shut inside the gates, Mack tore around the outside of the pens and took up his position at the dipping trough, frantic with expectation, waiting for the chance to leap into action again. One by one John seized the rams by their curled horns and flung them into the antiseptic. They would struggle to climb out the side, and Mack would snarl and snap at their faces to force them back in. Just as they were about to climb up the ramp at the far end, John caught them by the horns with a wooden implement, spun them around, forced them under again, and held them—ears, eyes and nose submerged for a few seconds. I've had some experiences in my life which have made me feel very sympathetic to those poor rams—I couldn't figure out any reason for the treatment I was getting from the Shepherd I trusted. And He didn't give me a hint of explanation. As I watched the struggling sheep I thought, "If there were some way to explain! But such knowledge is too wonderful for them—it is high, they cannot attain unto it." So far as they could see, there was no point whatsoever.

When the rams had been dipped, John rode out again on his horse to herd the ewes which were in a different pasture. Again I watched with Mari as John and Mack went to work again, the one in charge and the other obedient. Sometimes, tearing at top speed around the flock, Mack would jam on four-wheeled brakes, his eyes blazing but still on the sheep, his body tense and quivering but obedient to the command to stop. What the shepherd saw the dog could not see—the weak ewe that lagged behind, the one caught in a bush, the danger that lay ahead for the flock.

"Do the sheep have any idea what's happening?" I asked Mari.

"Not a clue!" she said.

"And how about Mack?" I can't forget Mari's answer:

"The dog doesn't understand the pattern—only obedience."

There are those who would call it nothing more than a conditioned reflex, or at best blind obedience. But in that Welsh pasture in the cool of that summer morning, I saw two creatures who were in the fullest sense "in their glory": a man who had given his life to sheep, who loved them and loved his dog, and a dog whose trust in that man was absolute, whose obedience was instant and unconditional, and whose very meat and drink was to do the will of his master. "I delight to do thy will," was what Mack said. "Yea, thy law is within my heart."

# 2

*Absolute Trust*

The glory of God's will for us means absolute trust.

Did Mack's response to John's commands hinge on the dog's approval of the route his master was taking? Mack didn't know what the shepherd was up to, but he knew the shepherd. Have you and I got a Master we can trust? Do we ask first of all to be allowed to examine and approve the scheme? The Apostle Paul admitted the limitations of his own understanding. "Now we know in part," he said. "Now we see through a glass darkly." But he was absolutely sure of his Master. He never said, "I know why this is happening." He said, "I know WHOM I have believed. I am absolutely sure that nothing can separate us from the love of God" (2 Tim. 1:12).

We start, then, with the recognition of who God is. He is our Creator, the one whose spoken Word called into being the unimaginable thing called space, which scientists tell us is curved, and the equally unimaginable thing called time, which the Bible tells us will cease. This is the God who dreamed you up, thought of you before light existed, created you, formed you, and now calls you by name.

When the Apostle John was an old

man in exile on an island called Patmos "on account of the Word of God and the testimony of Jesus," he was granted a vision of "One like a Son of Man"—eyes like a flame of fire, voice like a waterfall, face shining like the full strength of the sun—and in His hand He held seven stars. Old John, who had known and loved Jesus, was overwhelmed. He fell at His feet as one dead. And then the hand that held the seven stars was laid on him and the voice that was like a thundering cataract said, "Fear not, I AM—the first and the last. I died, I am alive, I have the keys. Now write what you see." What John saw turned out to be the Book of the Revelation, the most abstruse of all the books of the Bible— full of bowls of wrath and bizarre beasts, of lightning and harps and smoke and seas of glass and rainbows of emerald. The courage it took to put all that down in writing for other people to read came from the vision John had had of who it was that was asking him to do it.

It is this same One who asks you and me to do what He wants us to do: the God of Creation who's got the whole world in His hands; the God who in the Person of Jesus Christ "for us men and for our salvation came down from Heaven and was made man and was crucified." Those hands that keep a million worlds from spinning into oblivion were nailed motionless to a cross. For us. That hand that held the stars—laid on you. Can you trust Him? Two thousand years ago Paul said that the Jews were looking for miracles, the Greeks were seeking after wisdom. Not much has changed, has it? People are still looking for instant solutions, chasing after astrologers and gurus and therapists and counselors; but Christianity still has only one story to tell—it's an old

old story: Jesus died for you. Trust Him.

Karl Barth was once asked to sum up in a few words all he had written in the field of theology. This was the sum: "Jesus loves me, this I know, for the Bible tells me so."

# 3

## *Will to Do His Will*

If you can trust that kind of God, what do you do next? You do what He tells you. You obey. This was the second thing I saw when I watched the shepherd and his dog. If you know your master, you will do his will.

We identify ourselves with Christ or we deny Him. Jesus chose a path and went down it like a thunderbolt.

When we say as Christ did, "I have set my face like flint to do His will," we are baptized into His death; and like the seed which falls into the ground and dies, we rise to new life. "We have shared His death," Paul wrote to the Romans. "Let us rise and live our new lives with Him. Put yourselves into God's hands as weapons of good for His own purposes." I like that hard clear language: *put* yourself. Obedience to God is action. I can't find anything about feelings in the Scriptures that refer to obedience. It's an act of the will. "Our wills are ours," wrote Tennyson, "to make them Thine." God gave us this precious gift of freedom of the will so that we would have something to give back to Him. *Put* yourself in His hands. *Choose. Give* yourself. *Present* your bodies a living sacrifice. Until you offer up your will you do not know Jesus as Lord.

There are many who have made

this choice and said the eternal Yes to God—"Thy will be done." But you are wondering how you can know what it is that God wants you to do. If you can just figure out what the orders are, you are willing to obey them. You wish with all your heart that it was as clear to you as the pillar of fire to the children of Israel or the little metal whistle to the collie dog.

When the author of *Christ the Tiger* was a small boy, he used to pull out of the cupboard the paper bags that his mother saved and spread them around the kitchen floor. This was permitted on the condition that he collect them and put them away when he finished playing. One day his mother (who also happens to be my mother) found the bags all over the kitchen and Tommy in the living room where his father was playing the piano. When she called him to pick up the bags there was a short silence.

Then a small voice: "But I want to sing 'Jesus Loves Me.'" My father took the opportunity to point out that it's no good singing God's praises while you're being disobedient.

The epistle of John puts the lesson in much stronger language. He says: "The man who claims to know God but does not obey His laws is not only a liar but lives in self-delusion."

To will to do God's will involves body, mind, and spirit, not spirit alone. Bringing the body under obedience means going to bed at a sensible hour, watching your weight, cutting out the junk food, grooming yourself carefully (for the sake of others). It means when the alarm goes off, your feet hit the floor. You have to *move*. You may remember hearing of Gladys Aylward, a remarkable little London parlor maid who went to China as a missionary. She spent seven years there in happy single life before an English couple came to work near-by. As she watched them she began to realize that she had missed out on something wonderful. So she prayed that God would choose a man for her in England, call him, and send him straight out to her part of China and have him propose. She leaned toward me on the sofa where we were sitting, her bony little index finger pointing in my face, and said, "Elisabeth, I believe God answers prayer. He called him. But he never came." It's a little like the alarm clock—the call to duty. But *you* have to put your feet on the floor.

Bringing the mind under obedience means, for example, doing that reading your professor has assigned. The will of God for a student is to study. Being in college puts you under a set of obligations. You must pay your tuition, you must go to classes, you must write that term paper. You don't need to do any praying about whether you ought to do these things.

Being a Christian puts you under certain obligations, too. You are the salt of the earth, the light of the world—"My witnesses," Jesus said. You don't need to pray about whether this is your job or not, but bringing the spirit under obedience entails plenty of praying for understanding and for guidance about the how, when, and where. The Bible won't tell you whom to marry or what mission field to go to; but I believe with all my heart that as you seek honestly to do the things you're sure about, God will show you the things you aren't sure about. We might as well admit that most of our difficulties are not with what we don't understand, but with what we do understand.

In preparation for writing the book *A Slow and Certain Light,* I read through the whole Bible to find out how He guided people in those days. I found that in the overwhelming majority of cases it was not through what we'd call "supernatural" means—voices, visions, angels, or miracles—but by natural means in the course of everyday circumstances when a man was simply doing what he was supposed to be doing (taking care of sheep or fighting a battle or mending fishnets).

Just before he issued the Emancipation Proclamation, a group of ministers urged Abraham Lincoln to grant immediate freedom to all slaves.

"I am approached with the most opposite opinions and advice," Lincoln wrote, "and that by religious men who are equally certain that they represent the Divine Will. I am sure that either the one or the other class is mistaken in that belief, and perhaps, in some respect, both. I hope it will not

be irreverent for me to say that if it is
probable that God would reveal His
will to others on a point so connected
with my duty, it might be supposed
that He would reveal it directly to me;
for unless I am more deceived in myself than I often am, it is my earnest
desire to know the will of Providence
in this matter. And if I can learn what
it is, I will do it. These are not, how-
ever, the days of miracles, and I sup-
pose it will be granted that I am not to
expect a direct revelation. I must
study the plain physical facts of the
case, ascertain what is possible, and
learn what appears to be wise and
right. The subject is difficult, and
good men do not agree."

Lincoln said, "I must study the
plain physical facts of the case." If the
case happens to be the matter of be-
coming a missionary, you have to believe that God has something to do
with your even considering such a

career. He may call to your attention preparation you've already had that you never thought of as being for a missionary career. You may seek the advice of godly people whose wisdom you need. You look at a particular need and you see that you could in fact fill that need. The timing is right. "My times," said the Psalmist, "are in thy hands." You have certain gifts, given to everyone according to His grace, for the sake of others. Circumstances may point the way. Even your own desires could be sanctified and used for God's purposes. Paul had a streak of romanticism in him, I think, when he said that he wanted to preach where Christ had not been named. Why shouldn't God make use of a streak of romanticism? Study the facts. Use your head. Trust the Shepherd to show you the path of righteousness. Remember, nobody can steer a car that is parked.

One week before I graduated from college I learned that a young man named Jim Elliot was in love with me. I had been pretty sure for several months that I was in love with him, but kept telling myself that it would be fatuous to imagine that he could ever look twice at me. He was what we used to call a BTO—Big Time Operator—while I was a TWO—Teeny Weeny Operator. Furthermore, he was popular and attractive, and I was sure that every little sign that he might be interested in me was only my desperately wishful thinking. But no, he told me he loved me. My heart turned over and then sank like a stone when he went on to say that he hadn't the least inkling that God wanted him to marry me. He was going to South America, I thought I was going to Africa; each of us had just been through months of heart searching in an attempt to accept the possibility of life as a single missionary. We believed we had reached that point, and then Wham!—here we were in love. How do you discern the will of God when your own feelings shout so loudly? We prayed the prayer of Whittier's hymn:

*Breathe through the heats of our desire*
*Thy coolness and thy balm,*
*Let sense be dumb,*
*Let flesh retire,*
*Speak through the earthquake, wind,*
     *and fire,*
*O still, small voice of calm.*

We prayed Amy Carmichael's prayer:

*And shall I pray Thee change Thy will,*
     *my Father,*
*Until it be according unto mine?*
*But no, Lord, no—that never shall be,*
     *rather,*

*I pray Thee blend my human will with
  Thine.*

And one evening as we talked about
what was at stake, we agreed that it
really was too big for us to handle.
God's call to the mission field was
strong. Our love was, if anything,
stronger. There seemed to be only
one thing to do—put the whole thing
back into the Hands that made us, the
Hands that were pierced for love of
us, and let Him do what He wanted
with it. If He didn't want us together,
that would be the end of it. If He did,
"no good thing will He withhold from
them that walk uprightly." We had to
believe that promise. Some of you
know the end of the story. We waited
five years. Then God gave us to each
other for two years. Does this make
the will of God even more scary?

# 4

*Joy*

The glory of God's will for us also means joy. It can't mean anything less from the kind of God we've been talking about. He made us for glory and for joy. Does He ask us to offer up our wills to Him so that He can destroy them? Does He take the desire of our hearts and grind it to a powder?

Be careful of your answer. Sometimes it seems that He does just that. The rams were flung helplessly into the sheep dip by the shepherd they had trusted. God led the people of Israel to a place called Marah where the water was bitter. Jesus was led into the wilderness to be tempted by the Devil. The disciples were led into a storm. John the Baptist, the faithful servant, at the whim of a silly dancing girl and her evil scheming mother, had his head chopped off. More than twenty-five years ago five American missionaries attempted to take the gospel to a group of jungle Indians who had never heard of Christ. On the eve of their departure they sang together that great hymn by Edith Cherry:

*We rest on Thee, our Shield and our
    Defender,
We go not forth alone against the foe;
Strong in Thy strength, safe in Thy
    keeping tender
We rest on Thee, and in Thy name we go.*

One of the men was Jim Elliot, my husband by that time, who had written in his diary when he was a junior in college: "Father, take my life, yea, my blood if Thou wilt, and consume it with Thine enveloping fire. It is not mine to save; have it, Lord, pour it out for an oblation for the world." Could Jim have imagined how literally that prayer would be answered? Months of preparation went into the effort to reach the Auca Indians of Ecuador. The men prayed, planned, worked, dropped gifts from an airplane, and believed at last that God was clearly showing them that it was time to go. They went, and they were all speared to death.

Five men who had put their trust in a God who represents Himself as our Shield and our Defender were speared. They were speared to death in the course of their obedience. Now what does that do to your faith? Does it demolish it? A faith that disintegrates is a faith that has not rested in God Himself. You've been believing in something less than ultimate, some neat program of how things are supposed to work, some happiness-all-the-time variety of religion. You have not recognized God as sovereign in the world and in your own life. You've forgotten that we're told to give up all right to ourselves, lose our lives for His sake, present our bodies as a living sacrifice. The word is *sacrifice*. In one of Jim's love letters—and his were different from most, I can assure you—he reminded me that if we were the sheep of His pasture we were headed for the altar.

But that isn't the end of the story! The will of God is *love*. And the love of God is not a sentiment in the divine mind; it's a purpose for the world. It's a sovereign and eternal purpose for every individual life. We follow the

One who said, "My yoke is easy"; yet His own pathway led straight to the Cross. If we follow Him, sooner or later we must encounter that Cross. So how can we say that the will of God leads to joy? We can't possibly say it unless we look beyond the Cross. "For the *joy* that was set before Him Jesus endured the Cross."

Last year my daughter and I had tea with Corrie ten Boom. As she talked about her own experience and that of my husband Jim she took out a piece of embroidery which she held up with the back to us—just a jumble of threads that made no sense at all. She repeated for us this poem:

*My life is but a weaving betwixt my God and me.*
*I do not choose the colors; He worketh steadily.*
*Oftimes He weaveth sorrow, and I in foolish pride*

> *Forget He sees the upper and I the underside.*
> —GRANT COLFAX TULLAR

She then turned the piece over. It was a gold crown on a purple background.

The dog doesn't understand the pattern—only obedience. As George MacDonald put it, "Obedience is but the other side of the Creative Will."

The will of God also means joy because it is redemptive and it transforms. It is redemptive, for it means joy not only for me as an individual, but for the rest of the world as well. Did it ever occur to you that by your being obedient to God you are participating with Christ in His death, and then in His redemptive work? Paul told us this: "We have shared His death . . . we are weapons of good for His own purposes." Your response helps all the rest of us. Obey God, for His sake first of all. Obey Him for your own sake—if you lose your life, remember He promised you'd find it. But obey Him, too, for my sake—for the sake of others. There is a spiritual principle here, the same one that went into operation when Jesus went to the Cross. It is the principle of the corn of wheat. The offering up of ourselves—our bodies, our wills, our plans, our deepest heart's desire—to God is the laying down of our lives for the life of the world. This is the mystery of sacrifice. There is no calculating where it will end. The bitter water, the wilderness, the storm, the Cross—all are transformed to sweetness, peace, and life out of death. God wills to transform loss into gain, all shadow into radiance. *I know He wants to give you beauty for ashes.* He's given me the oil of joy for mourning, the garment of praise for the spirit of heaviness.

Jim Elliot and his four companions believed that "the world passes away and the lust thereof, but he that doeth the will of God abideth forever" (1 Jn. 2:17 KJV). Another translation (*Phillips*) says they are "part of the Permanent and cannot die." In Jim's own words, by giving up what he couldn't keep he gained what he couldn't lose. Because of Corrie ten Boom's obedience and that of her family, through the hideousness of a concentration camp, because they looked not at what's visible but at what's invisible, hundreds of thousands have seen the light of the knowledge of the glory of God. Jesus had to go down into death and the corn of wheat had to be buried and abide alone in order to bring forth life.

The glory of God's will means trust; it means the will to do His will; and it means joy. Can you lose? Certainly you can. Go ahead and lose your life—that's how you find it! "My life," Jesus said, "for the life of the world."

What's your life for?